No COINCIDENCES GOD *with*

Jo An Dunn

ISBN 978-1-0980-2959-3 (paperback)
ISBN 978-1-0980-2960-9 (digital)

Christian Faith Publishing, Inc.
832 Park Avenue
Meadville, PA 16335
www.christianfaithpublishing.com

Printed in the United States of America

PREFACE

*I*n the sixth grade I had a wonderful teacher named Ella Strail. She was a listener and an encourager. Under her wing, I learned to enjoy writing just for the sake of sharing ideas.

I only completed a high school education, but I read furiously all my life. At age 63–64, I retired as a school bus driver. I now had time on my hands. In that time, which was about 2011, I took a college course or two. Who would think, but I really enjoyed the learning and discipline of finishing assignments. One of the courses was on writing instruction called, specifically, a spiritual topography class. To this day, I am not sure I successfully fulfilled the sought-for paper, however, it was applauded and commented on highly.

I went on my own, and for Christmas the following year, I produced a book for my grown children. This book held memories of my own life growing up and also some of their formative years. I was hoping the memories would be shared with their own children. When we moved to Clay, New York, several years later, I joined a legacy writers group. I then dug in and continued with our stories, yet more and more, they evolved to telling a story of redemption and change. Many friends suggested I really should put my work out there, but I took it as just kind encouragement and not much more. That was until I met some new people who were struggling in life and needed a hand up. I am now hoping that this small work of mine, that truly God has produced, will in fact help them understand that change is possible. Not only that, but so much change can occur as to be called a modern-day miracle.

I know the Bible ends, but I personally think the stories of all believers, if told, could fill our world with books!

I have tried to be true to all facts, however, have left out some to pare this down to a reasonable read. There are truly no coincidences with God. He has his plans from the get go, and one tiny step after another, he will lead, to get us to his destination; that is, if we will only follow him.

This book is dedicated to my Lord and Savior Jesus Christ. Special thanks go to all my spiritual leaders, family, friends, and prayer warriors over these last thirty-three years. My hope is all who read this small work will grow in understanding of God's ways.

FAMILY

*M*y mind was down and out and way over the top, discouraged by the year just passed. Blows had been dealt to my life. Some were self-inflicted for sure, but many were the result of a marriage, simply put, gone bad. So in 1973, after nine years of marriage, a seven month separation, and then a month-long trial run to put the mess back together again, we finally cried uncle and determined to end the marriage. This time, I was the one who stayed in the farmhouse along with our three boys. We immediately put the land and house up for sale.

A few days of advertising, and I had a knock at the door. The man said he had seen the ad in paper and was driving around. He wondered if he could see the place now. Mind you, as he was talking, he was looking me and my kitchen over. My mind went to, *Look all you want, buddy. Not everything here is for sale.* I had not been feeling well, so with less than a gracious attitude, I told him he could look outside all he wanted, barn included, but I was sick and puking and did not feel like showing the house.

In the house, we had no heat or electricity as bills had not been paid, and things were not in order or very neat. The boys slept in one room, which was really the dining room. I was in a double bed in what was the living room, and then there was a functioning kitchen with wood stove, which was our only heat. It was October, so nights could be cold. The plan was to sell the farm, and the boys and I would move to Rome, New York. That would make popping in to see the boys a more planned-ahead deal, and I would not yet have to face the neighborhood folks to be more fuel for their gossip.

The same man who had stopped before called ahead this time. He wanted to walk around some more, and would that be all right with me. "Yeah, sure" was my reaction. Nothing more nothing less. A few days later, he called to say he would not be buying the farm, but he liked walking around and wondered did I mind. By then, I had decided he was harmless, and when he came next, he even asked about the two older boys walking the field with him. I said fine, and off they went. I guess they were not out of sight before I was asking myself how I could possibly have thought that was okay? Naturally, in a flash, I picked up the sleeping son and ran after them. In the end, I felt somewhat silly over that as he next asked could he just chop some wood for us. When he visited a few days later, he brought us groceries. Likely, he wondered about our empty cupboards; coffee was easy enough to offer and serve, but there was not much in solid food stored anywhere.

Well, you can see a guarded friendship was developing, and as long as he kept his space, it was kind of good to have some company. I knew he was an okay guy about the time I started dozing off watching TV with him. The truth is, in my first marriage and visiting at my in-laws, I could never go to sleep like that unless I was in my own bedroom. My husband had two brothers, and football was a big thing that everyone sat up late for. Sleep in the presence of any man just felt too threatening to me, yet with this man—boom—gone, just like that.

It came time to move, and he asked if he could help. My response was my parents had a truck; we were all set. The day came when the house was sold, and so we were on our way. In the driveway comes this same guy, yet again. It did take us three or four trips between Osceola, New York, and Rome even with his help. I was just not on top of how rich we must have been in stuff!

One thing led to another over the next few months, and we became more than friends. I was still emotionally not on top of things, so neither of us was going beyond today in our thinking. Over Easter, when we visited my parents, even going to church with the whole fandamily, my mom asked me how serious the relationship was. Yet still, I really could not answer, except that I knew in my heart, *he was good to us*. asking almost nothing in return.

Peter was not the kind of man I was naturally drawn to. Funny to think how we were put together, and so much time had to pass before we, either one of us, could see beyond to another season and to think we, as a couple, might survive. Truly, we were products of the sixties, and watching other marriages failing and seeing so many relationships being so fluid all around us, it's a wonder that WE lasted. We now celebrate forty years of wedded life, with a little more than two years shared before that.

We lived in Rome for part of that time, and Peter was trying to buy a house. He never said for us, and being unsure, I never asked. I did not know it was to be "ours" till almost the day Peter expected us to move. That was just a picture of how we were in the communication department. So time went on, and when I finally felt ready to marry, Peter decided his thirtieth birthday would be the day. This was also April 1, known as April Fools' Day. It seemed appropriate to both of us, and that's when we sealed the deal.

The joke has always been that Peter met me through a newspaper advertisement! That he looked to buy a farm and did, but not that one. The farm, of course, was one very busy woman and three boys. God is good, and we have grown since then. We got better over the years in this marriage thing and the communication piece, and Peter has been my stabilizer and made such a difference in my boys' lives. We added two more boys to the mix. Now we call it a whole family!

Peter Dunn and JoAn at marriage—first row from top left to right: Peter, JoAn, our son Brett in my arms, bottom row: Travis, Paul, and Robert.

Peter Dunn and JoAn at marriage.

SIGNS

*M*y desire as I sit to write today is to get us all to think about our lives and the intersections of choices, and mostly, those small choices that are made along the way.

It was about 1984, when I was a sales person for the Mary Kay makeup products. I was merrily making my way to a dinner celebration of other ladies, who were also in sales. We were all competing to sell the most products in an area covering six or eight towns, products of skin adornments that many women seem to depend on. So for me, it was time to play dress up and strut my stuff and sell, sell, sell. Off to Chittenango I went, more than happy to leave husband and kids to whatever made them happy!

My second son Paul, who was about seventeen at the time, was to look after his three younger brothers. My husband, Peter, was home, but a long day of work often left him sleepy before the wood stove, and that sleepiness often overtook him as soon as dinner was over. It was late November, and Peter decided to go out but did not tell Paul where he was going.

For my three-year-old Jess, this was family time, and he particularly looked up to his tall, handsome, and kind older brother. When Paul went to get more firewood from the shed, Jess, of course, went with him. On the way back in, they discovered Jess's dad was in the garage. Jess went in with him, while Paul got another load of wood into the house. He went to get Jess who did not want to leave his dad, but Paul, who was in charge at present, was able to talk him into going in. That despite Peters encouragement that he could stay there with him. Now Jess stumbled up the steps into the house, but his brother just thought he was tired and ready now for bed.

Paul got Jess to bed upstairs and went down to the living room to sit by the fireplace and get warm. Time passed, and something told him to check on Peter. The light in the garage was off, but Paul opened the door, only then deciding for sure that Peter must have walked to the neighbors for a visit. He went in the house and sat down again.

Now the phone rang after a bit, and it was the neighbor who Paul thought Peter might be visiting. She asked for Peter or myself, at which point, he realized that Peter had not gone there after all. My neighbor was merely calling to apologize for my broken car mirror. Her son had run into the mirror while riding his bike just that afternoon, and she was willing to replace the damaged mirror.

Paul sat back down again, but the feeling that he needed to know where Peter was came on strong again. He told us later, in fact, that he was told to go check again. He went to the garage, called, but got no answer. Still, he decided to go in and turn on the light. He found Peter on the floor, face up and just staring, unable to move, not responding.

Now Peter himself thought he had had a stroke or heart attack, and as he lay on the floor, he repeatedly, in his mind, called out to God. He promised God that he would change his life, if only God would give him more time in this life.

Now Paul decided he had to pick him up and drag him out of the garage. At this point, Peter began to come to and throw up, or he tried to. Paul immediately went in and called the neighbor, who then called 911.

At about 9:00 p.m., I got a call at the restaurant to come home now! When I got there, the ambulance and police were in evidence, and they were heading for the hospital. I answered police questions as best I could and flew after them in my car.

On the ride in the ambulance, personnel were administering oxygen and were unable, until the hospital, to check his oxygen levels. Our policeman friend told us later that, even after all that forty-minute drive to the hospital giving oxygen, he had "body bag" numbers when finally checked at the hospital. They did not understand why he was alive while so many have died with the same or even lower numbers.

It was so frightening to think of our youngest son. and what could have happened. If he had stayed in that garage with his dad, this would have been a sad story. You see, it was carbon monoxide gas that almost killed my husband and would surely have taken the life of a thirty-pound three-year-old in half the time. My husband had been welding a gift for his own father for Christmas. The parts he was welding were okay together, but he neglected to think of the welder itself, which would send forth its own mix of gases that were not okay in that closed-in area.

We could see the set of circumstances that saved both him and Jess from death. We were so very thankful that God had heard and granted Peter's prayer for life.

So you might ask, did Peter's promise to God, while laying unresponsive on the floor, make any difference in his life? He himself would share with you that nothing changed. It would take another crisis happening and more time passing before he got to the place of obedience that God was directing him to.

Another time, another story.

I myself was finished with my career with Mary Kay. It was taking me away from family too much but, also, was a waste of other people's money as it was wrapped in ego, pride, and self-preservation, regardless of what money they spent. I chose not to be a part of that, though I do enjoy being clean and somewhat cared for, and I even continue to use small amounts of makeup.

My son Paul learned that nudges and hunches, as he called them, are important to listen to. It also mattered for him down the road at another crossing where it was totally important to stay focused. Even little Jess learned later that obeying the one in charge was showing respect and that authority for what it really is a safeguard for our lives.

My point in sharing this story with you all is, God will do whatever he can to get our undivided attention. I myself think he does the same for all of us as his Word says, his desire is "that none should perish!" Will you look now for your signs?

ANOTHER WAKE-UP CALL

*L*ess than one year after Peter's brush with carbon monoxide, we walked through another lengthy maze.

My son Jess, who was now four years old, was going to a babysitter for about six hours per day. Carol Randesi herself had children of her own and also cared for several other children. I was working for an alternative school called EIDOS (another way of learning). The building we were using was approximately a mile from the sitters.

Now several weeks prior to the day I wish to tell you about, my son Jess was stung by a black-horned white furry caterpillar up at our camp in Forrestport, New York. Jess immediately started to itch and felt uncomfortable all over. His feet were itching first, and then he got a rash all over. The caterpillar had gotten him in the palm of his hand as he tried to bring him from under the camp to show it off. My mother-in-law was present and had sense enough to bathe him in baking soda till the rash calmed down.

About a week later, he was stung by a flying bug of some sort while at Green Lakes State Park. In this instance, his leg immediately turned hot and fiery red. After four days of being red and swollen, I took him to the doctor, really only because a friend felt it needed attention of some sort. We were given Benadryl and a salve to apply as needed for swelling and itching. We were cautioned to bring him in if it did not improve.

A couple of days or weeks later (I am really not sure how long), the children were playing on the outside swing set in the sitter's yard. A bee stung my Jesse on his right ear. The sitter took him inside to doctor him, but when he complained of his feet itching, she immediately called me to get his medicine. Luckily, I had told her about his reactions and the visit to the doctor. Now again, thankfully, our sitter acted quickly, first calling her husband and then Dr. Osborn's office. She then rushed Jesse there, this almost as soon as she hung up from me.

I had to drive from work to our home three miles away, get his medicines, and rush back to her house. Her husband flagged me down at the doctor's office which was a turn before Carol's house. Panicked, I raced into the office. When I entered, I could not believe my eyes. Jesse's whole body was swollen all over. His little arms and legs were like inflated water balloons. He could only half see me, was obviously terrified, and his ear stuck out from his head so far, and the ear itself was so long. It was just totally unbelievable! I thought, even if he survives this, he will never go back to normal.

Our sitter Carol told us later that by the two-block drive to the office, Jesse was choking, completely unable to get air in. Dr. Osborn had to administer adrenaline to keep his heart beating and Benadryl shots to counteract the results of the venom. When I arrived, they were giving the second set of shots as he was filling up again that fast. Dr. Osborn could not believe that, on this day, he was back unusually early from lunch. Had he not been there, this would have been an impossible situation as time would have run out before any other help could have been reached.

Again, thankfully, Dr. Osborn knew us well enough to just treat Jess and worry later about a possible lawsuit. Another dose of both medicines were needed, plus four hours of watchfulness at the office, before we were allowed to go home. As I recall, we had to go back before that day was over for another shot.

We were told to keep giving Jess the liquid Benadryl for up to a week. Let me tell you, it was not that simple. We had to watch him in sunlight all season and continued the Benadryl for weeks, much longer than they thought. When fall and winter came, he could not sit next to the wood stove because if he became overheated, that ear and his throat would begin to swell again. We went back to that Benadryl so many times, quite honestly, I have lost count.

Everyone in our family and extended family, plus the neighbors, thought we should keep Jess inside, but I insisted he was a nature lover, an outdoor guy who was at his happiest there. I thought and said, if there is a God, that he would protect him. I also felt I should not curtail his life to protect and prolong it.

The doctors told us that they could not test nor desensitize until he was free of reactions, which took about one full year. When they did testing, it was discovered he was highly allergic to hornets and yellow jackets. For me, this was confirmation that God had been, and was still, watching over our Jess. You see, a yellow jacket had been discovered in his room during that waiting time. So much for keeping him inside as a safety precaution. Bees do get in, but our God alerted us in time, and that one was dealt with swiftly, however, not forgotten then nor now!

My husband, Peter, and I both knew the set of coincidences happening that saved Jesse's life were not an accident of timing or fate but another wake up call for both of us that stirred us to thinking deeply. Now it would be only months till we would have to make a decision both of us never expected to make.

Jesse Dunn age 4 my outdoor boy.

SALVATION, 1986

So at forty-one years of age, this girl was plucked out of the fire-filled furnace. I now wish to complete her story here for you. Much water had gone over the dam of life, and I was literally dying of inside sorrow. I had lost hope in all things that were supposed to be the streams of a contented life. Mind you, this was all through my own doing. I made wrong choices over and over and over again!

I had been trying to stop my incessant drinking for over two years. I even got a victory of six weeks free during lent one year but, sadly, made up for it the next few months. Every promise to myself was broken by five in the afternoon, no matter what the morning vow was. My husband, not knowing my struggle, was constantly trying to please me. One of his ways of doing that was to surprise me with a big bottle of real liquor which, normally, we could not afford. My usual drink of choice was a beer or wine which was affordable. I felt I could not waste his money, so I would work through each bottle, now just compounding my issues. Yes, Satan was alive and well and working through my man, though he had no knowledge of being used in that way. Just an example of the sneaky serpent at work.

Going back in my mind, I want to relate to you clearly how God never gave up on me. Many years ago, I had rejected his Son to the point of just not caring about my sin or what the heck God's Word said. I was brought up with the head knowledge, however, it did not reach my heart as actually being real! Rather, it was like the story of Santa at Christmas or the bunny rabbit who, let's face it, as a kid, was the real excitement at Easter.

I had actually now been contemplating an easy way out of this life but had three precious boys I did not want to leave in my ex-husband's care. I also had two other sons by my husband Peter to think of. Still, I must admit to having these thoughts and dreams on a regular basis.

My oldest son, who was eighteen or nineteen at the time, was a new born-again Christian, and he was attending a strong Bible-believing church in Massachusetts on Cape Cod. I was taking the boys there to visit Robert, and the plan was to visit two days with him and then spend the rest of the week with my parents in Martha's Vineyard. On the way there, I was driving and drinking beer. In my trunk, I also had a bottle of wine and peppermint schnapps for later use that night.

Robert's church was just beginning revival week on that Saturday night. We were invited to attend with him, and I consented to go. I listened to the sermon where a man was preaching about the streets in the barrio. The preacher had served a seven-year prison sentence in the San Quentin jail. He was a heroin addict who actually stole money to feed his addiction. The last straw for him was he stole from his own mother, and she pressed charges. This was money for her ticket back to her own country where she desperately wanted to return. Now in prison, this man came to Jesus big time and was on fire for all things of God.

That first night, we went for pizza after service, and when I went to order my beer, my son said, "Why don't you just have a Coke like everyone else." Strangely, I did concede to this, which is still a mystery to me as Bob telling me what to do was not normal in any way.

The next morning, Robert and his family were going to church early but gave me directions to find the warehouse they called their church. We got ready after they left and headed out to find our way there. Rounding the same few blocks over and over hunting the right building, I was so frustrated. I finally said, "One more time around here for this, and then I am leaving, and we will just get the boat to Grandma's now." This was not said calmly but shouted, with uncouth wording added for emphasis at just how upsetting this all was for me.

In the meantime, by now, I thought we were very late for service. As it turned out, when we finally found our way in, they were just starting morning worship service as their Sunday school had gotten over late. After service, I remember crying as we were out by the car, and my son was trying to calm me. He himself was so calm when I was off the charts, upset with all my life and everything in it.

We ended up going to a spaghetti dinner following service, and I could not get over how at peace and how friendly everyone seemed. We went home and rested then went back that evening for another sermon. As the preacher was preaching again about the streets and sin and people killing themselves, I sat up and listened more intently. He spoke of a mother of three going to her garage, purposefully hooking up a hose and doing herself in. I knew that my children, at this point, were my only real link to life. You see, my man and I frequently did not see eye to eye on more and more issues as time went on, and yet, we stayed together, hoping to make it work.

While in service, my four-year-old was doing all he could to distract me and others around us. My oldest son took him to the other side of the church so that I could really listen.

When the preacher gave a call to come forward, I just stood solidly in place, not willing that any should see me as a sinner. I was in such a desperate state and was trying to sort out how doing that small thing would change anything in my life. This negative thinking included my husband and his attitudes that seemed immovable. At this point, my elder son came beside me and very quietly said, "Mom, you have to humble yourself before the Lord." There was something about those very few words that sent me flying to the front. Once there, I fell to my knees, not caring if I lost all by doing this! I knew my sin was, as they say, as scarlet, and I began confessing and asking for his forgiveness. Another lady came alongside of me and was praying, but I could not understand anything thing she said. She was not speaking English, that's for sure. When she switched to perfect English, I was totally thrown off as I assumed she was a foreigner.

Now the preacher standing in front of us started talking about the Holy Ghost. As he talked, he walked up and down telling us, or anyone who would listen, to ask for his infilling of this free gift that the Bible speaks of. We were now standing, and as he talked, he walked up and down, telling us to listen well and respond. I can't remember all that was said, but I was convinced this man spoke truth. I totally forgot anyone else was there with me. When the preacher again said to call on the Lord, I screamed out "JESUS" at the top of my lungs. People laid hands on my back and, at this point, hearing was gone to all around me. The next thing I knew, I was on the floor. Such a feeling of peace came over me as I went down, yet I felt no bump.

My seven-year-old thought I was dead as he later said that I just lay there so still. I don't know how long I was down, but when service was over, someone asked me a question I could not answer. The question they asked was, "Were you slain in the spirit?" For all of me, I had no clue what they were talking about. Someone else came from behind and said, "Yes! You were." Following that, they explained to me what "slain in the spirit" meant.

We went to Robert's after that service, and between the boys and I, we decided to stay for the 4–5 days of revival and only visit the grandparents for two days. This fact was startling as we would now only have two days with my parents and at our happy place which was on the island. In the meantime, on the telephone, I could not say much to my husband except that something needed to be talked about when I returned to him. Remember now, I had been trying for two years to stop drinking. That night, I went back to our place and poured all the schnapps, wine, and leftover beer right down the drain. Let it be known that for twenty-five years thereafter, I never touched a drop. Jesus had delivered me from that dragon which had been pulling me down for thirteen years.

Now my problem was to go home, quite possibly, to divorce proceedings. Strangely, at the same time, my husband knew something major had happened to me. When I got home and finally told him face to face, he just kept saying he knew. I told him I would like him to commit to going to church with me three times. I asked that he do that before making any decisions. In the meantime, my joy was obvious to many. I was often asked, "What happened to you? You look different."

Peter did go with me, and each service brought him more tears. In between, however, he seemed unable to talk about what was happening to him. He knew he had promised God during the carbon monoxide incident that he would change. He also knew that, indeed, nothing really had changed in him during the year that followed. On the third service, he went up front with me and committed his own life to Christ, so much so that, two weeks later, we were baptized together.

I forgot to tell you earlier that, while I was at the church in Massachusetts, they wanted me to be baptized right away. I insisted I wanted to wait for my husband. I am so glad I did as there is another story to that. It is so interesting to see how Good works in his time, his way!

Salvation is offered to all as we believe on the life and death of Christ to cover our sins? It is just too simple, and we fear being duped again, but God comes through, and we are saved!

BAPTISM

*B*efore I begin, I must first tell you that when Peter and I got married, we already had a son together. My mother-in-law wanted us to have a wedding with a minister as opposed to a justice of the peace. We wanted it small and quiet, but in deference to her wishes, we had her pastor officiate and were married in my in-laws' home. Celebrating with us were some of the family and a few close friends. When my mother-in-law had a girl from her church choir come to sing, she wanted to know what songs we would like. I clearly said, "Oh, whatever you choose is fine with us." She did a great job, and I will get back to that later.

Peter and I had been saved three weeks apart and, immediately, knew we needed to be baptized. We both had been sprinkled—he at birth and me at about ten—which was really a dedication of our parents to raise us in the Christian faith. In the Bible, it clearly states that at baptism, you must understand that you are a sinner and admit you are and commit now to live for Jesus.

So we, Peter and I and about ten others, got ready to be baptized, and this was in no certain order. We would just go forward to be dipped, one after the other. Peter and I wanted to go under at the same time, and we had arranged for that ahead with the pastor.

Now the congregation was singing song after song as each person went forward to testify to Christ having redeemed each of us. The pastor would speak over us as we were immersed. We did not realize the song had ended before we went under. It was to our delight and surprise that, as we came up out of the water, they were singing "Amazing Grace." Now this was the same song sung at our wedding, and let me tell you, the goose bumps rose. We were truly wretched sinners deserving of death, and instead, we were washed because of Jesus's blood shed for us. Years had passed since our wedding, but God has his way of teaching us how closely he watches over us. Again, it was no coincidence that "our" song rose for this momentous occasion.

The running was now over for us, and we dug into his word from that day to this. It is now thirty-three years later!

BUSING

*I*n 1988, two years after saying yes to Jesus, I left a lucrative job with a state-run program. I decided to give notice when attention was centered on Planned Parenthood. This attention was given in response to discovering one of our students was with child. Equal time was requested to have a Christian-based organization called New Hope in to speak with our students as a whole. This request was denied, citing separation of church and state. This organization offered adoption or real assistance with all it takes to care for a baby when girls end up in these unplanned situations. It was just too much for me to sit back, knowing abortion offered through Planned Parenthood was not the only answer.

I gave notice in April and left in June at our term's end. They tried throwing me perks to stay on and continue teaching employment skills, but I knew they would not follow through or back me in situations that, in my mind, had concrete answers to be looked at more closely.

I worked in a factory for a few months but saw an ad for a local bus driving job through our local school system. I immediately applied. Usually, a new hire would substitute drive for a year or two. This would mean an unsure paycheck and no joining the union till the worker was a full-timer. In my case, they determined that they now had a need for a contracted sub. This meant, every day, I would have work—if not driving, then I would be washing buses or cleaning in the garage. This extra duty rarely happened. Now I could join the union and have all benefits! For two full years, I jumped from bus to bus, route to route. Seriously now, really think about that! My dependence on the Lord for patience, endurance, and calm was constant. Without him it would have been impossible. Eyes on the road, eyes in the back of my head for behaviors on the bus—this meant a certain amount of in the moment every moment. Often without names and relationships that develop on a regular route, I was at the mercy of the ring leaders on any given route.

Twenty years later and many different routes lasting two to six years, I was ready to rest. I had done all the sport routes I could, in addition to my regular three- to six-hour days. Many days driving and also working, cleaning for other families, I found myself working more than eleven hours.

Who would have known, starting that job at forty-three, I could end up with a pension, health care, including dental and monies saved during those years. The Lord had taught me not only to tithe but to save, and now I see it has a purpose. I am able to share what I have with many. Without him, I would still be waitressing and house cleaning for others just for our own bread and milk.

Praise our provider who never ceases to look out for our welfare!

"MY CARS"

In the beginning of my "real Christian life" or, shall I say, the infancy of my actually following the Lord, I noted that God spoke to me most clearly through my cars. My first-time purchase of a dependable car, meaning one not more than five years old, I was divinely led. I found a Volkswagen Jetta that had been previously owned and well cared for. Being nervous about a long-term car payment and getting into a $7,000-debt payment was a very big deal for me. I prayed about that decision long and hard first, then decided if the bank said yes, that I would go for it. This was a big first hurtle as I had, in my previous marriage, acquired debt beyond what we could pay. Starting out on my own with three young children was not easy, but when I married again, I had worked hard in the town to establish good credit. I was hoping that, someday, I would be able to borrow in my own name once again.

When I got the bank's go ahead, I told God I had two other questions I would like answered concerning whatever car I chose. I wanted God to let me know who owned the car and why they had sold it. Surprisingly, the bank passed me through for a loan, and I then found the car I was interested in. Now I bought this car fifteen miles from my home and at a used-car dealership that got their cars from many different sources. I did not press my dealership for any information on this issue, but on the day of the pickup, I was glad I had my son with me. As we rode home, I asked him to check the glove box for a book on the car's maintenance. Inside the book was a name I recognized, and the information was from a dealer over in Rome, New York, where I had lived and worked several years back. A phone number was given for a man named Peter Blake, and when I called, a woman answered. When I asked if her name was Diane, and she said yes, I could hardly believe my ears! You see, I was a waitress at the Unwind Inn, and Diane and I had, for a short time, worked together. Since then, thirteen or more years had passed, and she had married this Peter Blake. Peter also did odd jobs at the restaurant along with his brother, so you see, I knew for sure who I was talking with. When I asked why they sold the car, she, Diane, lamented how much they missed it. However, she said they now had a third child after a skip of several years, so with the two older boys, they also had all of the baby stuff traveling with kids brings. The Jetta was no longer big enough for them, so they had traded it in for a van.

From that experience, I learned to trust God. Since then, I always pray before going into any new large purchases, and the Lord has so blessed those prayers. Many years have passed since then, and I thank my God continually for his leading of me. I am now on my fourth Jetta, my last being the most special. This time, I had talked to my dealers about what I wanted in my next car. On my list was: I wanted a red car, a sun roof, a good sound system, and I preferred a standard shift. We agreed on a price, but they came in $2,000 under my top price, and not only were all my wants fulfilled, but I had heated leather seats to boot! Sad to say, I have recently parted with this gem. She actually went 267,000 miles for me and was still running beautifully with little rust showing. Even that rust was strictly on the trunk area around the license plate only. We got nine years from her and sent her on to a young man just starting out his repairing skills and driving years.

Now I am not sure how God maneuvers such things to take place, but he certainly has shown me who he is in this trust relationship. He continues to bless in new ways as I learn to trust him more. If I did not have the initial experience of dependence on him while afraid to sign the first dotted line, think what I would have missed! Had I not trusted God's leading, I might even now be the one poo-pooing and saying, "Oh, that's just coincidence again!" Far be it from me as I am convinced we are taken care of as are the sparrows in the trees, just as his Word proclaims when it says we will be cared for. Faith is a wonderful exploration designed to last over our entire lives!

My cars

CAR MEMORIES

I have always enjoyed my cars and had many different ones over the years—once, a very float prone Bonneville Pontiac to a '54 Ford, a Simka, and then before it was over, with two different Corvairs.

It's the second yet older of the two Corvairs that I thought about today. My first husband and I bought a farm in Osceola, New York, in 1971, and it now became necessary for me to get back to the workforce immediately after my youngest was born. When he was less than six weeks old, and my other two were five and seven, it was off to work I went.

This old Corvair was a two-toned green 1960 rust bucket and was headed for the scrapyard but for our twenty-five-dollar rescue and a little work. I then lined up a baby sitter just down the road. (And the fun began!) I recall that start time for work was seven each morning at Harden Furniture factory in McConnellsville, New York. This meant a forty-minute commute in August and September and maybe into October, but as soon as the snow fell, it was much longer than that. Getting three little ones up and moving at that hour was no easy task. It was, however, left to me. My husband, who worked at eight in Syracuse, just could not take the responsibility of dropping the boys off just a bit later to make it easier for me. I learned to upholster furniture, which was a man's job previously, and I was only the second woman there to do so. I regret to say I only lasted till April; the five days a week and a half-day Saturday was just too much for me. I had even hired a live-in helper which relieved some of the preparations and running, but my days often ended in a beer fog. I just kept trying to keep up the pace, but I could not.

Still, when the work day was over, we would go for rides in that old Corvair. No seat belts in those days. and actually, the back seat floor was rusted out, so we had a board covering it. In one memorable trip, the three boys and I were out to visit a friend. One of the boys hollered something, but it was the second cry that I finally heard, "STOP! Travis's feet are touching the road! STOP!" He was unharmed as his brothers were holding him up as best they could, but that incident scared us all beyond words.

Another time driving along, a deer ran in front of us. I was sure we would hit him, but at the last minute, he flew over the top of the car! Well, he tried to anyway. His hooves hit the top and side window as he tumbled and rolled into the ditch. We stopped, all of us thinking him surely dead, but after a few minutes of no movement, he shook himself off and bounded for the nearest trees. We four stood outside the car, amazed that all in the world was still safe and sound.

When I left my husband and that Corvair behind, his girlfriend moved right in and drove my twenty-five-dollar gem all over town. I might say, "As if *she herself owned that car*!" I left in February but returned in September, trying to piece the marriage together but, within a month, gave up on that. After I finally retrieved my car and removed her stink from it and the house, we put the farm up for sale. When that parting came, it became a permanent thing, and the house sold quickly, and the boys and I left the area.

Interestingly, I came into that marriage with a *fully paid-for* shiny new red Corvair. It was an automatic with the stick on the dashboard. Within a year, the husband wanted to trade cars. Ever after, for the full nine years, it was the same story—a different car every year. Funny, I can't remember what he was driving in the end; maybe that Triumph, which was only made for two people of course. I, however, went off with just my green Corvair, my kids, and $250 in my pocket. Best of all, I knew I really meant it when I called myself lucky!

GOD SMILE

*O*nce upon a time, when I felt hungry for more of God but was stuck in a rut, I took it into my head to attend a do called 6 Days Ablaze, which was being held at another church forty minutes from us. I mentally committed to myself even if I had to attend alone to go for all six days.

Now I worked as a bus driver and also cleaned 4–5 houses a week for others at the time. Also, I had a husband and two boys still living at home, and believe me, they expected meals as usual. That week, I would also have to say no to extra sports trips and the extra pay to be made doing those trips. I still must arise at 5:30 a.m. to drive my regular route. I had read that this was for reconciliation, and that a local black choir would be there for the first night.

It was initially disappointing to see only two or three black folks in the audience, but the night was good and the music great. I kept asking friends to join me, but no one could or would spare the time, so I went alone. I believe it was the second evening that a voice called out my name behind me, and it turned out to be a young woman I grew up with who recognized me despite thirty years of not seeing each other! This was such a picture of the pleasures that heaven holds that, as we danced around hugging and laughing, I could not help feeling it was my glimpse into the unknown. Each night, "extra hands on prayer" was held for those who would stay late. The lines were long, but the wait was well worth it, and I was strengthened by it. I would get home at midnight and arise with elation the next work day. On the third or fourth night, I spotted a young man going forward, the same age and look as one of my nephews, and it excited me to see so many young people committing to Jesus early in life. I had been forty-one before salvation, and much of my life was so wasted.

On the sixth and final night, my husband, seeing my enthusiasm and knowing the cost, decided he would come with me. I still think of it as a magical night to this very hour.

As we drove into the parking lot, someone drove in from another direction and headed for the exact parking spot I headed for. I backed out and gave it up to them only to have my husband grumble about us being there first and on and on. When we got out of the car, I spoke to the two girls and, knowing they had not been there before, told them how to get a good seat and which door to go in to have the best chance of fast entry. We split up and shot for our seating only to discover it was already full, and they were now calling for the overflow room. We hung back and hoped the girls would do the same as I knew the ushers would get people to squeeze in to make more space. One seat opened, and my husband told me to sit; he would stand by the wall. Next thing I knew, another seat next to me opened, and Peter was able to sit down with me. They called again for people to move bags, let saved seats go, and when I turned around, the two girls from the parking lot had space on the other side of me. We exchanged names and places of worship and a few other quick words, and then the program started.

I noticed that my neighbor's hands were chapped and thought she must clean for people as I do. Little did I know, she herself would explain that hand before the night was over. At some point in the evening, I leaned over to tell her that I had just recently found out my great-great-grandmother was black. She asked a few questions, and we went back to listening to the sermon. I had told them of the prayer lines after service and encouraged them to not miss out on that blessing.

My husband actually directed me where to go so I would be sort of following the girls through the large crowd, that being a blessing in itself as he knew my heart was to get to know, in a more personal way, about my ethnic origins. After all three of us had been prayed for, and we were wandering around, one of the girls came up to me and said she had a word for me. Were to God I could remember all of it, but it was way too long. My best memory of it was she said what I had longed to and discovered finally of who I am in the flesh, God was wanting to show me who I am in Christ and so much more of heavenly things. Then the girl said she had to go find her friend and leave. I no more than turned to locate my husband, and her friend came to me. She said she had something for me that God had told her she was to give to me. She then placed a ring, black and gold and beautiful, in my hand. I immediately said, "Oh no, I can't take this." But she said, "You must." She went on to explain that she had had an affair with a married man who gave her the ring. She had then gotten saved and broke off all contact with him but said, each time she tried to wear that ring, her hand broke out in a rash. At that point, I accepted her gift that God had directed.

I am happy to say we exchanged names and phone info, and I did meet with one of the girls afterward, in fact, more than once. I look forward to meeting again in heaven and fill in all the blanks in their lives since our last meeting.

I had a jeweler look at the ring, and he told me it was black onyx, worth maybe $50. For whatever reason, I knew it was not true. I had even assured him I was not interested in selling. Several years later, I took it to a friend in the business and, without telling the story first, asked what it was and its worth. Turned out to be blue sapphire and worth $400 or more. I now pray for the right granddaughter to leave it to, a precious stone in so many ways, with God's handprint all over it. For me, it is and was as sweet as warm honey poured over my head. Only God would know that black and gold have always been my choice in colors for all my jewelry. And think about how God maneuvered a meeting of these two girls and myself who were black sisters in Christ. They both blessed me so by just their mere presence that last night.

It is blue sapphire.

Looks like black onyx

OUR VANS

May 28, 2019

*O*ur first experience with a van was a 1960s blue Volkswagen van that all bonified hippy folks seemed to have at that time. This van traveled around within our family many years before it had to be retired. We were the last of the family to have it up and running for any length of time.

My best memory of that van was a trip to Martha's Vineyard of course, where else? We had my niece with us then and four of our boys, and I think my in-laws met us there for that week. Of course, all of the kids rode in the back on the flat bed with no seat belts, which was allowed at that time. Upon our arrival to Grandma's place it was discovered that our oldest son, Robert had come completely shoeless. When you have hardly ice cream money to spare this was a huge deal. We could laugh later but really how could you possibly forget to even bring shoes? I was not in the habit of checking on a ten to eleven years old for essentials when I had four younger ones to deal with and pack for.

Once coming home from my workplace at the restaurant, which was three miles from home, the engine fell completely to the ground on Route 13 on a curve no less. After some fast scrambling and rolling of the van to safety, I got help from a friend to contact husband. We did still drive her after my father in law wired the engine in place and installed some tin to secure her staying there. Eventually she broke down completely and became a relic of the past. We parked her in our cousin's backyard where she still stands to this day.

We later acquired my parents van and paid the rest of the payments due on it. That van held for many years and when sold was still usable. We mostly reserved use of our vans for longer trips especially in the summertime. I must also admit that when making bread in spring or fall the van would catch the perfect amount of sun and heat up enough to aid in the rising process for bread! A van is also a very good place for busy mothers to retreat. Especially when a friend visits, where we could talk without extra ears running in and out of the conversation.

The time eventually came however when we were spending too much to keep that sad worn out van from running. I had been looking to upgrade for over a year, in fact almost two. I had nearly given up hope of a decent van within our low budget, one that would last for any length of time that is.

In 2009, I had swine flu, followed by pneumonia, then a six-day stay in upstate hospital. That was in October. In December I was still out of work and recovering way to slowly. One day, however, I spotted an ad for a conversion van with just 12,000 miles. It was said to have been kept in a heated garage and had all sorts of other bells and whistles on it.

I called the number and explained to the gentleman I would have to wait on my husband coming with me as I had been ill. I asked if anyone else was interested and he indicated one other party was but had not come up with any cash. I said we would come as soon as Peter got home from camp.

When we got to his place the owner said he had gotten the van for his father for his trips to Florida but that his Dad did not really like it. He only used it for two trips south and then it sat indoors till we were looking at it. The day we went to see it was stormy with snow flying, and we were in hilly country. Not good! Still it was so perfect, and was selling for unbelievably just 10,000 dollars. It was also in pristine condition. We gave him money down to hold it till I could beat feet it to the bank for the loan.

Once the deal was struck and when paperwork was in hand, I still wondered if at the motor vehicle department we would be told it had a hold on it as a stolen van. Praise God everything went smoothly and was just as he said.

We have had many trips and wonderful times in that wagon with all its trappings and space. They even left the sheets and blankets on the bed, as well as the rugs on top of the carpet and lastly a nice pair of high heels were included. Oh, I forgot the plug in cooler which my in laws had more use for as they took more trips cross country in their own van.

This purchase was made at Christmas time, unemployed to boot, however we knew how God had blest us before in many different things. We determined since it was a God led thing, that we would have the faith to expect the finances to juggle into place to meet all loan deadlines. By that time in life our credit was good and all fell into place with no problems from the start of the deal to the last payment.

Now ten years later, we are still driving this van and in reality it is still worth the 10 grand we paid originally. We are ever so thankful for Gods hand in our lives.

Our newer van

THE MAN

*F*unny how some memories are easy to write about, and everything flows in a logical fashion. This particular story is not like that—a work situation, a married man, a problem needing intervention, and I, also a married woman, with a need for a defense which called for our bus driver union leader to step in.

The problem called for unusual time spent together for the president of the union and myself to map out the defense and how to go about fighting for the right outcome. In my mind, God won the case for us. Being the woman of God I was and wanting my friend to have a clear sense of who I am in heart, I gave all credit to God. I wanted so much for this gentleman who walked through the trouble with me to understand my strength was not really mine.

Time passed. We would sometimes drive our buses to the same sports events and, there, whiled away the hours together. Now the subject often turned to God. I was never sure just why, but at one point, he did indicate that he felt our friendship was meant to be.

That spring, my friend had the opportunity to get a job in his hometown, which was fifteen miles south of us, thus eliminating the travel he was now doing just to get to and from the bus garage. I found it interesting that he came and asked my opinion on the move. I knew I needed to encourage him, but how hard it suddenly was to think of him gone from my everyday life.

The next fall, he was not with our fleet anymore, and by that October, I was missing him more. I mentioned this to someone else and even said how strange it was that his absence left such a hole. Well, as things go somehow, that was repeated to him, and he called to ask if I would go for coffee. I spoke with my husband for guidance and then agreed to meet him in a very public place and, thus, began a new relationship. I remember being very up front with him as in actually saying, "I have nothing to give you but Jesus." If I have my timing right, we would talk off and on for the next two years. Our talks were usually over coffee and mostly midday, between our driving assignments. A year and a half after we began meeting this way, he accepted Jesus as his own Lord and Savior and admitted *that Jesus was now ruler over his life.* He told me, even his kids who were all grown knew he was different.

That spring, he brought me a flower catalog and asked me to pick out a favorite color rose. This I did, not realizing its impact. Now for a year, I had been falling on my knees before the Lord about this man—yes, for his salvation, but also because I knew who he was inside, and I loved him. Always, he had a smile for *everyone,* never picky in the who's who area. He always wanted to talk if he thought there might be a problem, not just with me, but everyone he interacted with had this same treatment. It did not matter if it was a five-year-old or a seventy-year-old, he had interest and time. He was also a humble man and knew his mistakes in this life were great.

Now fall came again. He would call and say he needed to see me. I grew to hate this "need' word and felt unsure what my response should be. Our last day together, he had a pale peach rose for me; it was blooming on my table when I got word he had died of an aneurysm.

I never saw such a funeral as there was for "That Man." There was a literal choir loft filled with every child on his bus from five- to eighteen-year olds, all present and accounted for. It was too much for this weepy lady to witness and hide so much feeling, but I tried not to stick out in the crowd.

Need I tell you, my grief seemed bottomless; it was so very deep. Yet, I had a husband and family to care for and a job to continue performing, always being ever so careful to remain in the moment. Sorrow does not evaporate in a night. Two years later, I was still crying—crying out to the Lord that no one loved me like that man, no one would ever give me roses again, and other such depressing thoughts. Within two hours of that out-loud statement to myself and God alone, a young man I did not know and never did see again walked up to my bus. He bowed low and said, "I don't know why I am doing this, but this is for you." From behind his back, he pulled a beautiful peach rose, royally presenting it to me as if I was truly Queen for the Day. I laughed and I cried, trying to tell him about my friend, and that these were happy tears. Finally, I had release of the sorrow. I could now see God listening to my cries and was deeply caring for me in a very personal way.

I am happy to say, my husband of forty years has now stepped more into his role in these last few years. His attention to me proves to me that God is still working on all his broken vessels. No coincidences here that I can see, NOT!

DIFFERENT FORKS ON
THE ROAD OF LIFE

*L*ately, I have been thinking about the fact that when we are born, each of us are equipped with talents and experiences that build on each other. These attributes prepare us for the next chapter we will find ourselves in. Growing up in the United States of America, which is sometimes referred to as the melting pot of humanity, we all are exposed to different cultures as we go about our business of the day.

Starting out in Newton Highlands, Massachusetts, which was, at that time, pretty white and tight, I would have been quite sheltered. That is, except for the fact that we spent part of each summer on the island off the East Coast called Martha's Vineyard. That—in the '40s, '50s, and '60s—introduced me to African Americans, Portuguese, and Native Americans of the Wampanoag tribe. I remember it was terrible to move to Camden, New York, at seven, where again, it was all white, and to me this was boring. However, when I was about fourteen, our churches had gotten together and helped a family to immigrate and settle on a farm just outside of town. I recall that the family was from Russia and had many children. Shondor Horvaith was my age, and he had a sister close in age, so we spent time with them. I visited at their home and was intrigued trying to talk with them. They had homing pigeons, and I loved watching them and dreaming of the messages they must be taking to others a long way away that the family knew.

When I later moved to New Jersey with my first husband, there were many Jewish families around us who had come from Germany. They were not very friendly, for some reason, but I would overhear the strange language on the streets and in the shops. Again, in that area, there were many African Americans, but in 1964 and all through the '60s, it was best to avoid those areas where riots often broke out.

In my very young years, before I became jaded over organized religion, I wanted to go to Africa to help people. Back in the Sunday school days of giving and dreaming life, I seemed to have more heart. I won't say it completely disappeared, but I no longer held on to the illusions of childhood. However, we have an advocate, and he is not giving up.

Not long after Ken and I were married, my brother-in-law, who was serving in Germany, wrote that he was marrying a local girl. She would be coming home with him at his discharge and was now carrying his child. Christa knew very little English when I met her, but she had a desire to continue as a hairdresser in our country. This meant she needed to pass tests and show her stuff on a model, and I was it. We spent time together that summer, and come fall, they moved up north where my husband was in college. Now both brothers were going to Canton (ATC), under the G.I. Bill, and we spent much time together. In relating to Christa, I had to patiently try to help with her English and find ways to communicate when speech did not work. Years later, I had a new daughter-in-law who was also from Germany and was a challenge to always understand.

By this time, I was in my forties and had become a born-again Christian. About four years along in my Christianity and fourteen years into my second marriage, we were in another church, our second one. We began to get *au pairs* coming to visit our place of worship. The first girl that was placed with a local family came as a Christian herself but brought in three others who practiced no religion. Over time, in befriending them, I learned that in Germany, Hungary, and the Czech Republic, the churches were mostly like empty shrines to these girls. They said they were more like ancient museums, where few attended service. I also realized most people around me would not take the time to try to communicate with these young girls. I guess they did not think how far away from home they were, nor how lonely they were sure to be.

In all, we had seven young ladies, mostly eighteen to twenty-one, come through our church, all of whom became, for a time, part of our family. These girls were so hungry for connection and care that I simply could not understand how the rest of our church family could not see the need that was right there before them. We would take them on family trips to Martha's Vineyard, the lake, or our camp in Forrestport. The best thing was that they had a renewed interest in the Bible. I say renewed because at least two had some Catholicism in their childhood days. I will never forget Nina and how she finally understood why they call Jesus the

Lamb of God. It was exciting to capture their awe as prayers we had prayed together were answered. Their host families were most often off in their own work worlds, and the girls coped with children and, usually, a dog to walk and clean up after as well. When vacation times came, the family packed up and left these girls adrift, without much in food store, and no pay while they were gone. So we would gather for some meals and evenings together and talk about their dreams and homes and families and maybe boyfriends. We really missed them when, after one full year, they would go home and be replaced with yet another girl. Our church took a turn in a down slide when a pastor arrived who was not really qualified for the position. So our time with that sort of ministry was cut short after three years.

We then began with a church in Cicero, New York, that was an offshoot of the Cape Cod church I was saved in. The first year, a Native American got marvelously saved, and that same year, a girl from the Rwanda massacres joined us as she was attending Syracuse University. In our second year there, we began to have an influx of people from Nepal who were still Hindus but had one family member who was a Christian. We started with maybe three families and, at one point, had a congregation of about seventy, with only maybe fifteen to twenty being Americans. The young Nepalese who had been in camps for eighteen years were translating for the older folks. They would translate the sermon, which required patience on both ends and then extra time to work on the language barrier after services.

During this time, I was still driving school buses, but the Lord helped me manage my time wisely. I was in and out of

Syracuse on the north side four or more times a week. I had a Bible study for the woman and helped them shop, especially helping to locate secondhand shops and Indian food outlets. Many families lived together and, being used to life in camps, did have a way of leaving their mark. I don't think, to this day, gum wrappers or the like ever hit a trash can, at least, not until thrown on the ground and picked up a second time by someone else.

My husband and I claim two women as our adopted daughters. One family now lives in Ohio, but we still hear from them. Aksana, my granddaughter in that family, calls me, now that she turned six, just to chat. She told me last week that when she gets big, she will drive a car and will come to see me often then.

My other daughter has three children, and her oldest has graduated with a two-year college degree. I expect the other two are as capable and will also be well educated. They are all good people, and we have received back much more than we have given.

We really feel that though we lost out on becoming real missionaries out of country, that God gave us missionary work to do right where we are. Ours was with foreigners in our own country, not outside of the United States, and they are now part of us. Many American people I find shied away from dark skin, different body odors (which is due to the food we eat), and also others ideas different from what they grew up with. We want to be a bridge wherever we are and to all people.

Those who choose not to see the need or don't take time to understand have missed so much. We even brought living goats into our backyard to be carefully killed and processed, to go back to the city for neighborhood feasts. We watched as the woman prepared intestines to be used later. The men knew to bury the remnants and clean up without enlisting our efforts at all. My mother-in-law had a mixed blend of peoples praying for her at her bedside in her last days. My adult children may not have wanted us so tied up with these others, but they saw what was happening and, by our example, have seen the blessings that go with giving.

I don't know why the world is as it is, except without Christ, we can be like animals. With an understanding of the living Christ, we strive to be more than we are naturally. We have watched each family come to have real relationship with Jesus, each other, and with us. They find jobs, buy cars, and buy homes eventually. Eternity awaits, and we will die before most of those friends, but we look forward to our reunions in heaven.

JoAn Dunn, Peter Dunn, Tika, and Dilip Chapagai

Jesse Dunn, Peter Dunn, our extended family
Tika Chapagai and Dilip Chapagai

Chapagai Family

Ramesh Wagle's graduation from college. Sisters
Chali and Aksana with his dad Kana Wagle.

Mom kala, Ramesh, and Kana
Wagle now living in Ohio

Another family with extended
generations: The Tamang family.

GIFTS

*I*t would seem that 2018 was our family's year to really shine. Nothing like a small Christmas gift to show you how things have moved the good meter of life forward for an extra big jump!

My husband and I each lost our parents within the last eight years. We were still working through family moves, paperwork for three different estates, and monies to settle out. So to say the year 2018 was good is quite the surprise, especially for me.

Still, when the year turned from 2017 to 2018, I decided to move forward as if we had no cares to worry over. A one-week vacation at a house on the island of Martha's Vineyard was secured. At that time, all five of our boys and their children were invited to share the rental with us. We ended up feeling so cared for and blessed as all these faith-based plans fell into place.

So sight unseen, we signed the agreement on said house, along with a one-night necessary stay at a motel on our way there. Both of these, the house and motel, were sights unseen. Each of the three cars and all the passengers needed boat reservations. We could not get those at the same time, however, we could all get the same motel. The day finally came, and the fun began.

Two of our sons got to the motel first and were amazed
to find how perfect it was for all. Picture a square set way
back from the main road, with an open plot for cars and
bike riding or play for kids, That and in back of each unit
was grass space and play area for children to race around
in. We each had a deck to share between two rooms and
an inside sitting area apart from the bedrooms. We were
able to join together for dinner on the double deck and
watch the kids wear themselves out on the green in front
of us. Once tired, each had their own family unit to go to
for sleep. We saw only two other people go in and out of
their rooms, but it was so peaceful and quiet. Having been
in many motels, it was a blessing we will not soon forget.

Two families left real early for the ferry, and we old-
sters got off later. The early risers got to Martha's Vineyard
first and got to swim and see all the sights before the house
became ours for the week.

I totally wish I had recorded the excitement of all as
they each tried to be the first to show my husband and I
and our son, who lives with us, what exactly we had for
our enjoyment for the whole week. This home had three
complete floors, four bedrooms, two full baths, and a third
smaller one. Not only that, there was an in-law apartment
which meant there were two kitchens. This was necessary
as we needed two refrigerators to house enough food and
drink for fifteen of us. There were two separate decks with
entry for each, two outdoor grills, a porch in front which
could also seat all. This area was great for early morning
coffee. We, of course, had a den, living room, dining room

and, in the basement, a large room with couches and television and room for energetic kids to play.

This brings me back to my gift! I am reminded of the turkeys coming each and every morning to entertain both the children and the adults. Corn was purchased before the end of the first day. This assured us that the turkeys would return, and did they ever! Sometimes, they came three times per day. Then one day six to fifteen came at a time. They tried to climb the porch stairs following corn in little hands. The kids were definitely afraid when this happened.

My nephew Chris, who is an islander himself, has always been into cars and does many shows all over the country. He joined us many a night and, on one, brought his beauty, a 1931 Ford Coupe, and some were offered a ride to the downtown area. So much fun for all. He is meticulous in the care of all his cars owned over the years, so it must have been another hour or two of cleaning after our rides. It was so much fun, and to have him visit nightly after a hard day of work was a blessing in itself. Good for cousins to reacquaint themselves after many years going their separate ways. Chris managed to take a day at the beach with us also.

Of course, we spent much time on the beaches, and with so many choices, it was sometimes together, and sometimes split from the crowd. No thanks for me on those six in the morning beach times that kids love so much. I did that for many years but now prefer to sleep in and, after coffee, cook until the families gather midmorning.

In conversation, back at the motel, I, Grandma, had stated that "I can still stand on my hands in the water." My son Brett said, "Ha, fat chance of that. The last time I tried it, I really hurt my back, and it lasted for days." He is more than half my age, but I still insisted I could do it. The kids, of course, were cheering the debate on, so of course, I had to prove it. Yup, the picture shows there I am, with feet in the air, for all to see, and that at seventy-three years of age. Here's cheers to us all. Now it is down for history to see, and since I do all the writing for the family, I have taken care to get it down in print too!

My grandson Jackson and his sister Molly have recently moved from Arkansas to Louisiana. We only get to see each other once or twice a year as, unfortunately, there had been a divorce. Jackson is eleven and pretty laid-back and quiet until you spend some quality time playing his way. Then he opens up and becomes a guy determined to hold his own in every situation. We were able to play games on land and in water, and it was fun to watch him lead the three younger kids in good play at every opportunity he was given.

Molly is everyone's friend. She is a beauty, but I want to concentrate her attention to becoming good inside, and it is fun to encourage all that at every turn. She now has a younger brother in the other family, and it is my hope she will learn many ways of becoming a good woman. She and I have much in common, and having missed out on my older two granddaughters, I do not want to lose touch with Molly.

In another family, we have Max at five, and Ryan at seven. Of course, I would say both are great boys, and they really are. Being close in age, they are always competing with each other. When they play together, it is awesome to watch all their interactions. My prayer is despite the personality differences, that they will always be good to and for each other.

Since my oldest son and his family did not come to visit us, it meant the oldest grandson there was Zac. He is eighteen and had just finished up his freshman year in college. At that age and station in life, family times are not so exciting for him. Zac spent a good part of his time with us sleeping or on social media or, otherwise, off in his own little world. Another few years, and his head will be on straighter.

The best thing about the week was, within three days, my boys started talking about next year doing the same. Even after seven full days together, they felt the same, so before another week passed, we put in our bid for 2019, and already, it is secured for July 14–21.

We are spoiled as, in the meantime, we, or rather, my son now owns my in-laws' camp, which has two cabins and is located up near Forrestport, New York. We go up there when we can, but two of the boys are there weekends whenever they can. They go more in spring, summer, and fall but, some, for snowmobiling in winter.

When my son Travis has his kids for a month in summer, they go to this camp for part of the time. It is a great place for dirt, dune buggy rides, four wheelers, and campfires. The great thing is he has, in 2018, found another woman who shares his interests and passions, and it seems the children even feel she is a great stand-in for Mom while they are with Dad. Sonja herself is a new grandma and has a daughter with a child and another on the way. She is just naturally great with kids, a very good cook, and knows how to please her man. My husband would tell you, those attributes are the things a man wants most in his mate. So after much sadness in his life for so many years, our Travis is finally the fun guy we used to know.

My son Jess, who is with us these days, is enjoying all the family times and, this year, has shown improvement with a change in medication. Our hope is this may be the year he can get back to a more normal life. We are fortunate that his health, as well as our own, is pretty stable these days.

Back now to my Christmas gift that brought all these memories to the forefront of my mind, this would be the gift given by one of the families.

Of all the things we received at the holidays—gift cards to spend, CDs to listen to, games to play, not to mention food, dishes, and clothes—of all those, my favorite gift was a mug! This mug has the pictures on it from the past year, just as I have described them for you here.

Travis's Sonja laid out the design for the pictures which are included and even put in one of Trav's dog, Maggie. All the kids are attached to her as she always goes to camp with them and loves it as much as they do. The mug is a treasure I will fill each and every morning. It will start my day in memory, yet give me courage to face the changes ahead that will bring both new joys and new sorrows for each new day. Hopefully, many more joys as we have had in 2018!

STRIKING OUT

*I*n the spring of 2017, I enjoyed a day at Syracuse Stage watching the play *A Raisin in the Sun*. This play left me thinking about race pretty much nonstop for days thereafter. My friend and I went early for the special talk before the show. Much information was shared on life in Chicago following the migration of people of color coming North looking for work in the 1930s. This migration soon created a housing shortage, and the play was written around this time to portray what it was like to be poor and black.

For me, watching this for more than three hours brought a long-suppressed incident to the surface for inspection. I had, literally, *almost* forgotten it!

In the fall of 1963, after graduating high school, I had been working in a nursing home. I honestly hated it there—the smells, the food, and the low mood of everyone there, including all the workers. It was catching even for a young woman of eighteen, and it began to make trouble in my stomach first. As I increasingly became sicker and sicker, I knew a change had to be made. In all, I lasted there only about three months, but that was much too long.

It happened that my old girl scout leader had a son who was a manager at a Hotte Shoppe restaurant in Saugerties, New York. This is a town east of Albany, about three hours from my hometown. I would be completely on my own there, but for me, that was exciting. In looking for a room or apartment to rent, there seemed to be many but none who would accept me. My father decided maybe a word from him would help open doors. With the additional help of a minister and Dad, I was moved into a small room on the second floor of a house. With just a single bed, one straight back chair, and a dresser, I had room to close the door and lay on the bed to stare out the one tall window. Still, for me, who was used to sharing a big house with five siblings and a business, this was a whole new start in life. Here, I had the use of a kitchen and an ironing board no less, all shared by others renting in this house. Not much, you might say, but for me, it was freedom of choice now—when to eat, when to sleep, or to play the radio on the station of MY choice.

Surprisingly, at that time, I thought my inability to secure a place to live was due to the fact that I looked too young. It would be another year before I felt the full force of having a questionable ethnic background. That would be a whole other story for another time.

In our preplay background talk at the theater, our speaker brought out that in America and across much of our land in those years, many sections were off limits for ownership or rental properties to people of color. These laws were written into contracts for sales of lands and homes on a regular basis. This ensured that people of color would not move in as your neighbors, but more than that, they would not marry your offspring.

It was many years before I knew that I myself was more than French, Indian, Scotch, and English. At the age of fifty, I learned that I had a great-great-grandmother who was black, was born in 1837, and had come up from Florida in 1855 and married a white man from Maine.

I am extremely grateful that education was very important to my grandparents and my parents because it is clear that, without education, we are at a loss to change with the society around us. Our ghettos are continuing to fill up with people who have not had the opportunity to learn and make a good living. Much anger is still rampant all these years later in these people left behind. Inner city living has not changed much, and it is very sad to understand that we have people living in this country who are shortchanged because hope is lost before they get started. The parents in these communities often fail to hold up education as the key. In addition, the inner city schools are not doing as well for these long-term citizens as they do for the new immigrants that we see and work with locally. To me, it is time to look seriously at this problem in our country. We need to shore up all of our resources, especially for our people living here for generations. Those who were brought, in many cases, against their will still need our help. So I am asking myself as well as you, what is our part in all of this? Where do we go from here? We need to make the starting line equal for all. I hope more will do the same soul searching as, without a way to live together with justice for all, we will eventually implode in our own country.

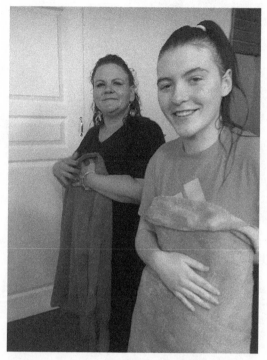

Deanna Stuper and her daughter Siera

Wanting to acknowledge Deanna Stupor a forty-one-year-old born again believer who, with her daughter, was baptized in Syracuse, New York in March 2019. She was the one who told me I must give this bit of writing in book form for everyone to read. Thanks for the encouragement girl!

ABOUT THE AUTHOR

*J*o An Dunn has been writing for about nine years. It all started when she attempted to write a book for her five sons for Christmas. She wanted to give a lasting gift rather than an expensive throwaway or some plastic nothings that we try to show love through. She began writing her story and their story, and then it took off to other memories.

In a writing group, her work turned more and more to personal spiritual material and memories.

In *No Coincidences with God*, her desire is that this small window into our lives will encourage others. God puts his footprints on our lives regardless of us seeing or acknowledging them. Hopefully, this will help others see that God can help even them, no matter their present condition.

Jo An recently moved from Cazenovia, New York, where she resided for forty years. She and her husband moved to Clay, New York, to the home that his father and grandfather built in about 1950.

Retirement leaves time for digging into old dreams and doing the best one is capable of with what you have learned through the years. Her hope is you will grow through this window of awareness.

9 781098 029593